INSIDE A
BADGER'S BURROW

By Rex Ruby

BEARPORT
PUBLISHING

Minneapolis, Minnesota

Credits: Cover and title page, © Ralf Geithe/iStock, © Voren1/iStock, © naKornCreate/Shutterstock, and © Jana Scigelova/Alamy; Design elements throughout, © pictafolio/iStock, © Antagain/iStock, © texcroc/iStock, © t_kimura/iStock, © Antagain/iStock, and © Croc80/iStock; 4, © zenaphoto/iStock; 5, © LAURIE CAMPBELL/Alamy; 6–7, © Buschkind/Alamy; 9, © Zeljko Radojko/Shutterstock and © Minden Pictures/Superstock; 11, © David Chapman/Alamy; 12–13, © imageBROKER/Horst Jegen/Alamy; 14, © Sylvain Cordier/Biosphoto; 15, © twildlife/iStock; 16–17, © Les Stocker/Alamy; 19, © Maciej Jaroszewski/iStock; 20–21, © Geoffrey Kuchera/Alamy; and 22, © legna69/iStock, © moose henderson/iStock, © leekris/iStock, and © Ildiko Laskay/iStock.

Bearport Publishing Company Product Development Team

President: Jen Jenson; Director of Product Development: Spencer Brinker; Senior Editor: Allison Juda; Editor: Charly Haley; Associate Editor: Naomi Reich; Senior Designer: Colin O'Dea; Associate Designer: Elena Klinkner; Product Development Assistant: Anita Stasson

Library of Congress Cataloging-in-Publication Data

Names: Ruby, Rex, author.
Title: Inside a badger's burrow / Rex Ruby.
Description: Minneapolis, Minnesota : Bearport Publishing Company, [2023] |
  Series: Underground animal life | Includes bibliographical references
  and index.
Identifiers: LCCN 2022006974 (print) | LCCN 2022006975 (ebook) | ISBN
  9798885091367 (library binding) | ISBN 9798885091435 (paperback) | ISBN
  9798885091503 (ebook)
Subjects: LCSH: Badgers--Behavior--Juvenile literature. |
  Badgers--Habitations--Juvenile literature. | Animal burrowing--Juvenile
  literature.
Classification: LCC QL737.C25 R83 2023 (print) | LCC QL737.C25 (ebook) |
  DDC 599.76/7156--dc23/eng/20220314
LC record available at https://lccn.loc.gov/2022006974
LC ebook record available at https://lccn.loc.gov/2022006975

For more information, write to Bearport Publishing, 5357 Penn Avenue South, Minneapolis, MN 55419. Printed in the United States of America.

Contents

A Secret Home

It's early evening in the **meadow** when suddenly, a striped face peeks out of a hole in the ground. The face belongs to a badger, and the hole leads to its **burrow**. All day, the badger has been asleep underground. Now, it will spend the night searching for food.

Badgers live much of their lives in burrows. They sleep, hide, and raise babies there.

A Badger's Body

There are different kinds of badgers in North America, Africa, Europe, and Asia. These chunky animals have wide, flat bodies and short legs. Most have thick grayish hair on their bodies and white-striped faces. Badgers dig burrows in open, grassy places such as **prairies** and meadows.

The largest adult badgers can be more than 4 feet (120 cm) long from nose to tail.

Building a Burrow

Badgers dig burrows with their shovel-like feet. First, the hardworking animals loosen the soil for an entrance with their sharp front claws. Then, they kick the soil out of the hole with their back feet. At the end of their long tunnels, they make a cozy bedroom!

A badger's bedroom may be up to 10 ft. (3 m) underground.

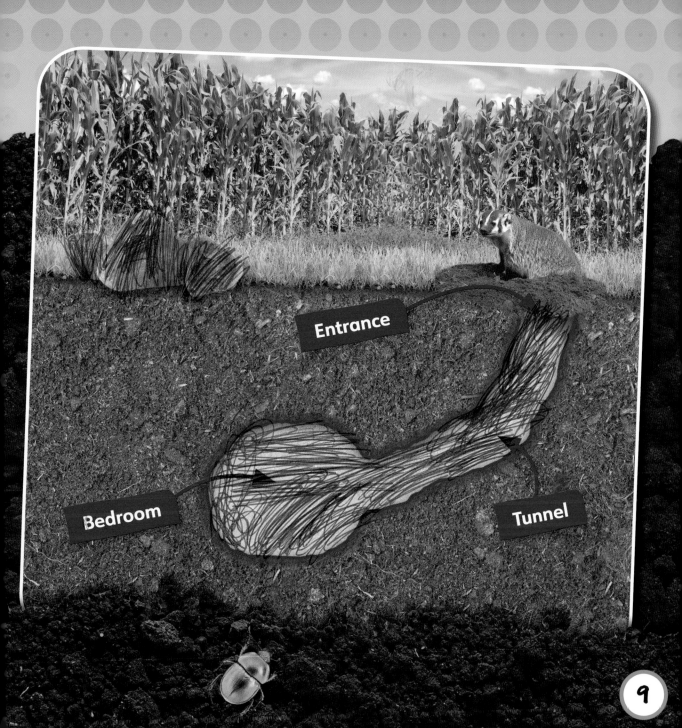

Sleepy Days, Busy Nights

Badgers are **nocturnal**, which means they're mostly awake at night. In the evening, they leave their burrows and may walk many miles looking for food. In the morning, when it's time to sleep, the furry animals find one of their burrows. A badger may have hundreds of burrows in the area where it lives!

Badgers usually leave piles of fresh dirt near the holes to their burrows

Digging for Dinner

Badgers eat plants as well as small animals, including bugs. Some badgers hunt for larger **prey**, too. When badgers find other animals underground, they dig down with long claws. The prey may try to dig away, but badgers dig faster. Often, badgers can catch prey that are trying to scramble deeper into their own burrows.

Badgers also eat fruit, insects, lizards, frogs, and birds' eggs.

Staying Safe

While badgers are powerful **predators**, they sometimes become prey. If a bear or wolf comes too close, a badger will try to hide in a burrow. But if the enemy catches a badger first, the badger will use its teeth and claws to fight. It also makes sounds to scare away the attacker.

A badger can dig a burrow backwards to get away from a predator in front of it!

Baby Badgers

Adult badgers usually live alone. However, they meet up to **mate**. In the winter or spring, a mother badger digs a burrow with a soft bed of grass inside. She gives birth to babies called kits. The mother badger feeds the kits milk from her body.

Badger kits are born with their eyes closed. They cannot see until they are about four weeks old.

A young
badger kit

Life in the Burrow

The new mother badger spends her days cuddled up with her kits in the burrow. At night, she leaves the babies safe underground and goes out to find food. When the kits are six weeks old, they leave the burrow for the first time. They are big enough to follow their mother while she hunts.

A mother badger gives birth to a **litter** of one to five kits at a time.

Growing Up

Baby badgers begin to eat meat when they are about six weeks old. The mother badger catches small animals for her babies. The kits also drink their mother's milk, for another couple of months. When they are about five months old, they are ready to leave their mother.

A badger usually lives for 5 to 10 years.

Be a
Badger Scientist

Badgers live in the same areas as raccoons, groundhogs, and opossums. These animals are often a similar shape or color as badgers.

Scientists must be able to identify an animal even if they can see only part of it. Which of these pictures shows a badger? What animals are in the other pictures?

The badger is D. A is a raccoon and B is a groundhog. The animal in C is an opossum.

22

Glossary

burrow a hole or tunnel dug by an animal for it to live in

litter a group of baby animals born at the same time to the same mother

mate to come together in order to have young

meadow a field covered with grasses and other plants

nocturnal active mainly at night

prairies large areas of flat land covered with grass

predators animals that hunt other animals for food

prey an animal that is hunted by other animals for food

Index

Read More

Labrecque, Ellen. *Day and Night on the Prairie (Habitat Days and Nights).* North Mankato, MN: Capstone, 2022.

Murray, Julie. *Burrows (Animal Homes).* Minneapolis: Abdo Kids Junior, 2020.

Sabelko, Rebecca. *American Badgers (North American Animals).* Minneapolis: Bellwether Media, 2019.

Learn More Online

1. Go to **www.factsurfer.com** or scan the QR code below.
2. Enter "**Underground Badger**" into the search box.
3. Click on the cover of this book to see a list of websites.

About the Author

Rex Ruby lives in Minnesota with his family. He doesn't live underground, but he would love to explore a badger's burrow if he had the chance.

Book O Time